# ACOUSTIC GUITAR RIFFS

ISBN-13: 978-0-7935-9292-0

ISBN-10: 0-7935-9292-5

HAL•LEONARD®
CORPORATION

7777 W. BLUEMOUND RD. P.O. BOX 13819 MILWAUKEE, WI 53213

Visit Hal Leonard Online at
**www.halleonard.com**

# CONTENTS

| PAGE | TITLE | CD TRACK |
|---|---|---|
| 4 | Angie – THE ROLLING STONES | 1 |
| 5 | Babe, I'm Gonna Leave You – LED ZEPPELIN | 2 |
| 6 | Behind Blue Eyes – THE WHO | 3 |
| 6 | Blackbird – THE BEATLES | 4 |
| 7 | Close My Eyes Forever – OZZY OSBOURNE WITH LITA FORD | 5 |
| 8 | Crazy on You – HEART | 6 |
| 9 | Dust in the Wind – KANSAS | 7 |
| 10 | Fast Car – TRACY CHAPMAN | 8 |
| 11 | Fire and Rain – JAMES TAYLOR | 9 |
| 12 | Foolin' – DEF LEPPARD | 10 |
| 10 | Free Fallin' – TOM PETTY | 11 |
| 13 | I'd Love to Change the World – TEN YEARS AFTER | 12 |
| 13 | Ice Cream Man – VAN HALEN | 13 |
| 14 | Landslide – FLEETWOOD MAC | 14 |
| 15 | Layla – ERIC CLAPTON | 15 |
| 15 | Love Song – TESLA | 16 |
| 16 | Maggie May – ROD STEWART | 17 |
| 17 | Melissa – THE ALLMAN BROTHERS BAND | 18 |
| 17 | More Than Words – EXTREME | 19 |
| 18 | Name – GOO GOO DOLLS | 20 |
| 19 | Norwegian Wood (This Bird Has Flown) – THE BEATLES | 21 |
| 20 | Pink Houses – JOHN "COUGAR" MELLENCAMP | 22 |
| 21 | Silent Lucidity – QUEENSRYCHE | 23 |
| 22 | Tears in Heaven – ERIC CLAPTON | 24 |
| 23 | Time in a Bottle – JIM CROCE | 25 |
| 20 | Wake Up Little Susie – THE EVERLY BROTHERS | 26 |
| 24 | Wanted Dead or Alive – BON JOVI | 27 |
| 25 | When the Children Cry – WHITE LION | 28 |
| 26 | The World I Know – COLLECTIVE SOUL | 29 |
| 25 | You Were Meant for Me – JEWEL | 30 |
| 27 | Guitar Notation Legend |  |
|  | TUNING NOTES | 31 |

# Angie

**Words and Music by Mick Jagger and Keith Richards**

Track 1

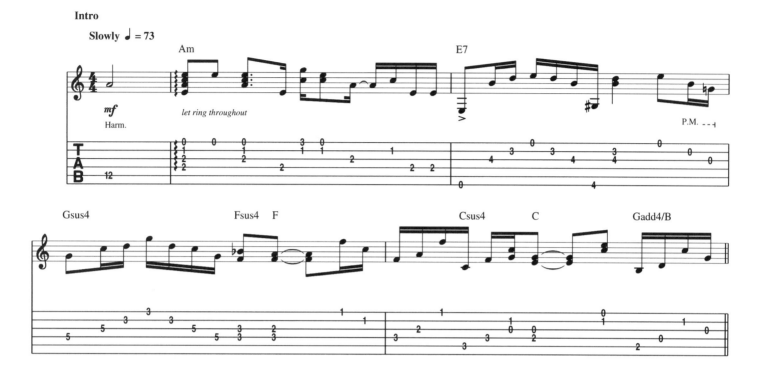

**Artist:** The Rolling Stones
**Album:** *Goats Head Soup*
**Year:** 1973
**Guitarists:** Keith Richards, Mick Taylor

**Trivia:** It is commonly believed that the lyrics to this song were inspired by David Bowie's first wife. However, the song is rumored to be about Keith Richards's common-law wife of ten years, Anita Pallenberg. Richards's and Pallenberg's daughter Dandelion renamed herself Angela.

# Babe, I'm Gonna Leave You

**Words and Music by Anne Bredon, Jimmy Page and Robert Plant**

Track 2

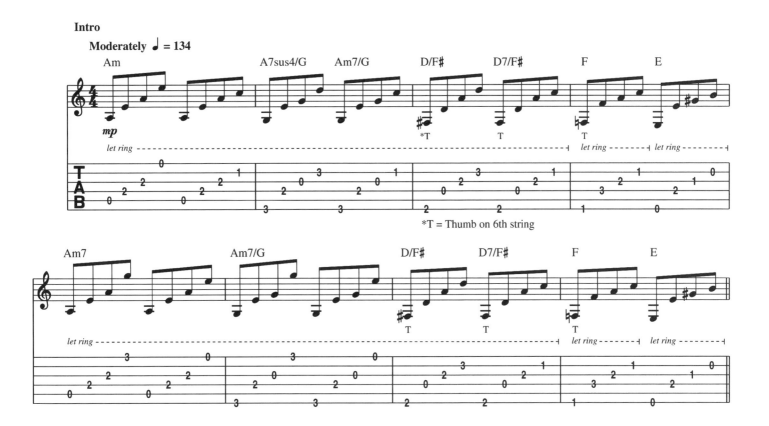

*T = Thumb on 6th string

**Artist:** Led Zeppelin
**Album:** *Led Zeppelin*
**Year:** 1969
**Guitarists:** Jimmy Page

**Trivia:** The songwriting credit for "Babe, I'm Gonna Leave You" on the original printing of the *Led Zeppelin* album falsely states that the song was "Traditional" and "arranged by Jimmy Page." The song was actually written by Anne Bredon, a folk singer who recorded the song in the 1950s.

# Behind Blue Eyes

Words and Music by Pete Townshend

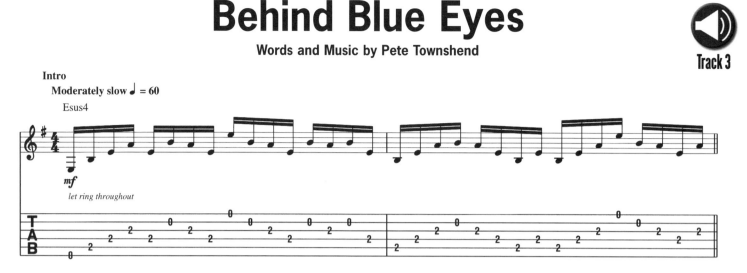

**Intro**
**Moderately slow** ♩ = 60

Esus4

*mf*
*let ring throughout*

| | |
|---|---|
| **Artist:** The Who<br>**Album:** *Who's Next*<br>**Year:** 1971<br>**Guitarist:** Pete Townshend | **Trivia:** "Behind Blue Eyes," as well as other songs from *Who's Next*, were originally meant to be part of an abandoned Pete Townshend multimedia conceptual work called *Lifehouse*. |

---

# Blackbird

Words and Music by John Lennon and Paul McCartney

Track 4

**Intro**
**Moderately** ♩ = 92

G          Am7          G/B          G

*mf*
*w/ fingers*

| | |
|---|---|
| **Artist:** The Beatles<br>**Album:** *The Beatles* (White Album)<br>**Year:** 1968<br>**Guitarist:** Paul McCartney | **Trivia:** The lyrics to this song are sometimes interpreted as being pro-black civil rights, and Paul McCartney has stated that he had something similar in mind when he wrote it. Unfortunately, Charles Manson misinterpreted this and other songs on the White Album as having hidden meanings. |

# Close My Eyes Forever

**Words and Music by Lita Ford and Ozzy Osbourne**

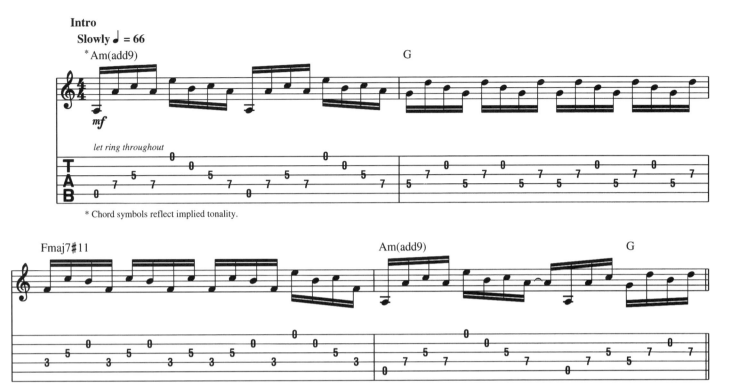

\* Chord symbols reflect implied tonality.

**Artist:** Ozzy Osbourne with Lita Ford
**Album:** Lita Ford - *Lita*
**Year:** 1988
**Guitarist:** Lita Ford

**Trivia:** Drummer Randy Castillo (1950-2002) has played in both Ford's and Osbourne's bands, but he did not play on this duet.

# Crazy on You

**Words and Music by Ann Wilson, Nancy Wilson and Roger Fisher**

**Artist:** Heart

**Album:** *Dreamboat Annie*

**Year:** 1976

**Guitarists:** Nancy Wilson, Roger Fisher

**Trivia:** This song, which was Heart's first Top 40 hit, has appeared on the motion picture soundtracks for *The Virgin Suicides*, *A Knight's Tale*, and *Harold and Kumar Go to White Castle*.

# Dust in the Wind

### Words and Music by Kerry Livgren

**Track 7**

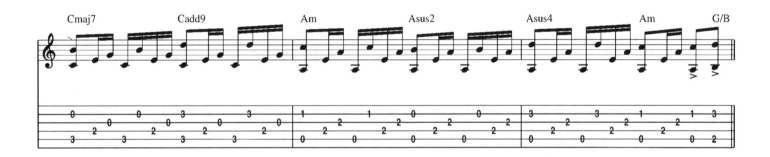

**Artist:** Kansas
**Album:** *Point of Know Return*
**Year:** 1977
**Guitarists:** Kerry Livgren, Richard Williams

**Trivia:** Kerry Livgren created the chord progression for this song as a finger exercise. When his wife heard it she told him it had a nice melody and he should write lyrics for it. "Dust in the Wind" turned out to be the band's highest-charting single.

# Fast Car

**Words and Music by Tracy Chapman**

Capo II

* Symbols in parentheses represent chord names respective to capoed guitar.
Symbols above reflect actual sounding chords. Capoed fret is "0" in tab.

| | |
|---|---|
| **Artist:** Tracy Chapman<br>**Album:** *Tracy Chapman*<br>**Year:** 1988<br>**Guitarist:** Tracy Chapman | **Trivia:** This song has been covered many times, and was even sampled for the demo version of British soul singer Gabrielle's song "Dreams." However, the sample was removed when the single was released in 1993 due to legal issues. |

# Free Fallin'

**Words and Music by Tom Petty and Jeff Lynne**

Capo I

* Symbols in parentheses represent chord names respective to capoed guitar.
Symbols above reflect actual sounding chords. Capoed fret is "0" in tab.

| | |
|---|---|
| **Artist:** Tom Petty<br>**Album:** *Full Moon Fever*<br>**Year:** 1989<br>**Guitarists:** Tom Petty, Jeff Lynne, Mike Campbell | **Trivia:** Tom Petty wrote this song after a roadie bought a keyboard that Petty didn't particularly care for. The roadie told Petty if he wrote one song on the keyboard it would pay for itself. The song did indeed pay for the keyboard, as it reached #7 on the U.S. charts. |

# Fire and Rain

**Words and Music by James Taylor**

**Track 9**

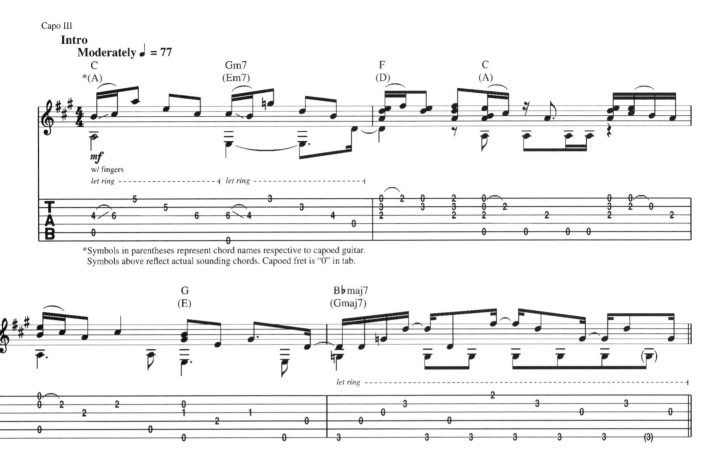

\*Symbols in parentheses represent chord names respective to capoed guitar.
Symbols above reflect actual sounding chords. Capoed fret is "0" in tab.

**Artist:** James Taylor
**Album:** *Sweet Baby James*
**Year:** 1970
**Guitarist:** James Taylor

**Trivia:** Many have thought this song is about the death of Taylor's girlfriend Suzanne in a plane crash.  However, the song is actually about multiple events in Taylor's life: the death of his friend Suzanne (though not by means of a plane crash), Taylor's heroin addiction, and his stay in a mental hospital.

# Foolin'

**Words and Music by Joe Elliott, Steve Clark, Peter Willis, Richard Savage, Richard Allen and Robert Lange**

Track 10

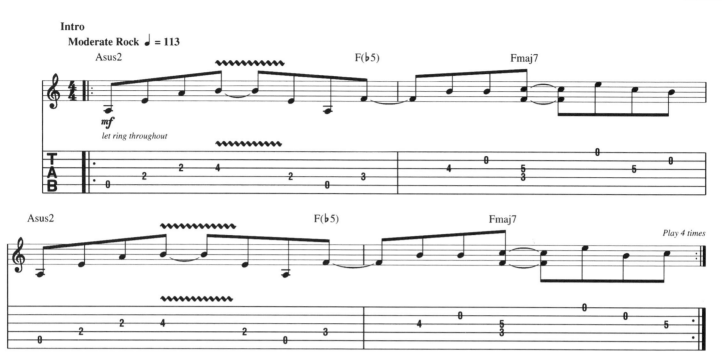

**Artist:** Def Leppard

**Album:** *Pyromania*

**Year:** 1983

**Guitarists:** Steve Clark, Phil Collen (Note: original guitarist Pete Willis was still a member of the band during part of the recording of *Pyromania*.)

**Trivia:** The *Pyromania* album is Diamond-certified by the RIAA, meaning 10 million copies have been shipped in the United States. The band's much-anticipated follow-up, *Hysteria*, shares the same honor, making Def Leppard one of only five rock bands to have two original Diamond-certified albums in the U.S.

# I'd Love to Change the World

**Words and Music by Alvin Lee**

**Track 12**

| **Artist:** Ten Years After | **Trivia:** "I'd Love to Change the World" received airplay on not only the free-spirited FM-radio stations, but also the pop single-oriented AM-radio stations of the early 1970s. This may be considered unusual for a band with heavy blues influences and a number of long songs. |
|---|---|
| **Album:** *A Space in Time* | |
| **Year:** 1971 | |
| **Guitarist:** Alvin Lee | |

# Ice Cream Man

**Words and Music by John Brim**

**Track 13**

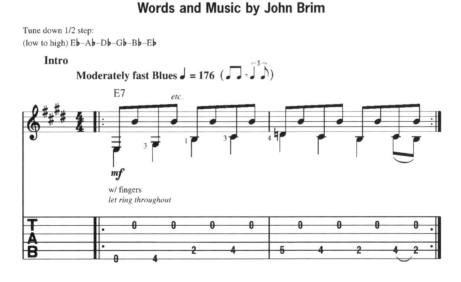

| **Artist:** Van Halen | **Trivia:** Due to its suggestive lyrics, the original version of this song recorded by songwriter John Brim in 1953 wasn't released as a single until 1969. |
|---|---|
| **Album:** *Van Halen* | |
| **Year:** 1978 | |
| **Guitarist:** David Lee Roth | |

# Landslide

## Words and Music by Stevie Nicks

**Track 14**

Capo III

**Intro**

**Moderately** ♩ = 80

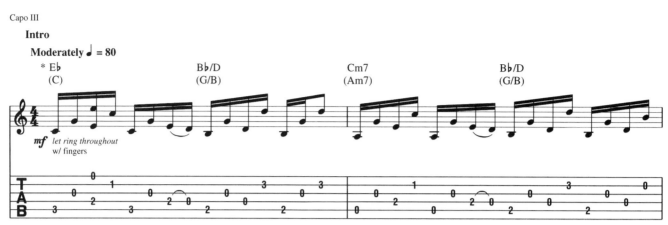

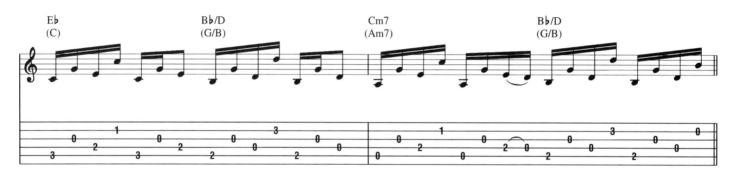

\* Symbols in parentheses represent chord names respective capoed guitar. Symbols above reflect actual sounding chords.
Capoed fret is "0" in tab. Chord symbols reflect implied harmony.

**Artist:** Fleetwood Mac
**Album:** *Fleetwood Mac*
**Year:** 1975
**Guitarist:** Lindsey Buckingham

**Trivia:** This song has been covered by artists such as the Smashing Pumpkins, the Dixie Chicks, Tori Amos, John Frusciante of the Red Hot Chili Peppers and Joey McIntyre.

# Layla

### Words and Music by Eric Clapton and Jim Gordon

**Track 15**

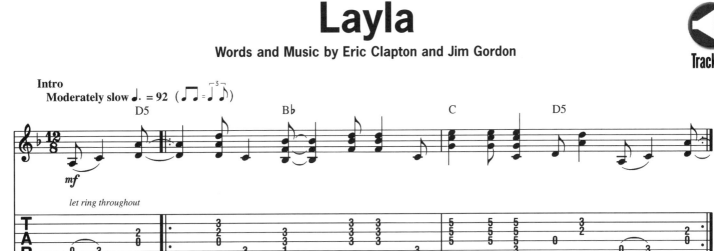

**Artist:** Eric Clapton
**Album:** *Unplugged*
**Year:** 1992
**Guitarist:** Eric Clapton

**Trivia:** This song's title comes from a Persian love story called *Layla and Majnun*, but the rest was inspired by Clapton's unrequited love for George Harrison's first wife, Pattie Boyd.

# Love Song

### Words and Music by Jeffrey Keith and Frank Hannon

**Track 16**

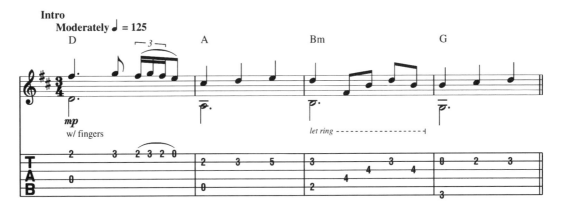

**Artist:** Tesla
**Album:** *The Great Radio Controversy*
**Year:** 1989
**Guitarists:** Frank Hannon, Tommy Skeoch

**Trivia:** Tom Zutaut from Geffen Records suggested the band adapt their name from electrical engineer and inventor Nikola Tesla, whose first major invention was the alternating current motor.  After his death he was recognized as the inventor of radio, though its creation is credited to Guglielmo Marconi, which influenced the album title *The Great Radio Controversy*.

# Maggie May

**Words and Music by Rod Stewart and Martin Quittenton**

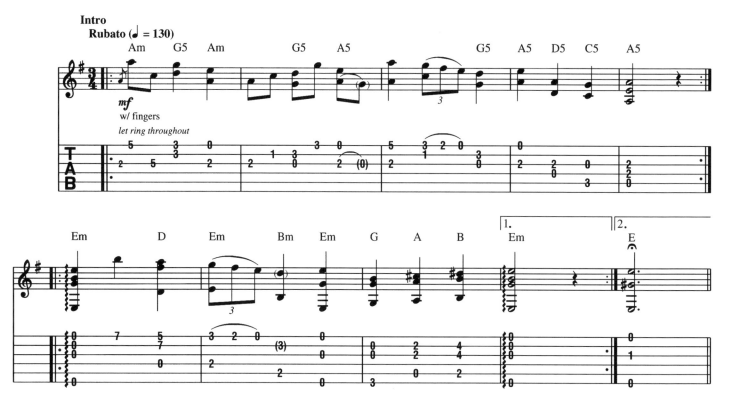

**Artist:** Rod Stewart
**Album:** *Every Picture Tells a Story*
**Year:** 1971
**Guitarist:** Ron Wood

**Trivia:** This autobiographical #1 hit was actually the B-side of the single "Reason to Believe." It topped both the U.S. and U.K. charts simultaneously.

# Melissa

**Words and Music by Gregg Allman and Steve Alaimo**

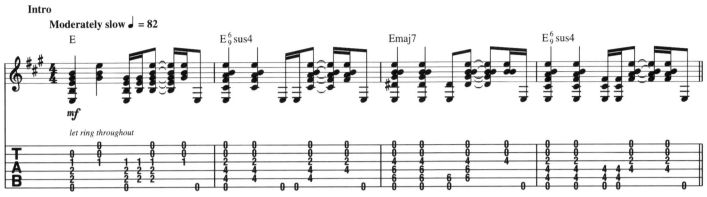

**Artist:** The Allman Brothers Band
**Album:** *Eat a Peach*
**Year:** 1972
**Guitarists:** Gregg Allman, Dickey Betts

**Trivia:** One popular story about the origin of the *Eat a Peach* album title states that the truck involved in Duane Allman's fatal motorcycle crash in 1971 was a peach truck. The truck that hit Allman was, in fact, a flatbed lumber truck.

# More Than Words

**Words and Music by Nuno Bettencourt and Gary Cherone**

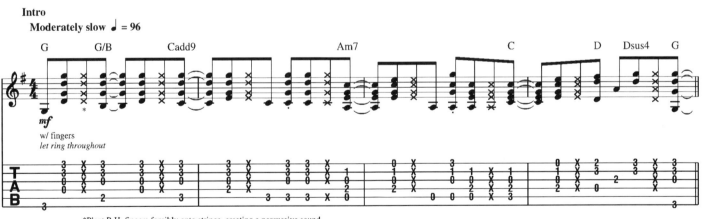

*Plant R.H. fingers forcibly onto strings, creating a percussive sound

**Artist:** Extreme
**Album:** *Extreme II: Pornograffitti*
**Year:** 1990
**Guitarist:** Nuno Bettencourt

**Trivia:** This ballad, which was a #1 hit in 1991, seems rather out of place on the *Pornograffitti* album – a hard-rocking concept album about a boy's observations in a decadent and corrupt society.

# Name

**Words and Music by John Rzeznik**

Tuning:
(low to high) D–A–E–A–E↑–E

**Artist:** Goo Goo Dolls
**Album:** *A Boy Named Goo*
**Year:** 1995
**Guitarist:** Johnny Rzeznik

**Trivia:** The name Goo Goo Dolls came from an ad in *True Detective* magazine. The band had to change their name from the Sex Maggots early in their career, otherwise a club owner wouldn't allow them to play.

# Norwegian Wood (This Bird Has Flown)

**Words and Music by John Lennon and Paul McCartney**

Capo II

\* Symbols in parentheses represent chord names respective to capoed guitar.
Symbols above reflect actual sounding chords. Capoed fret is "0" in tab.

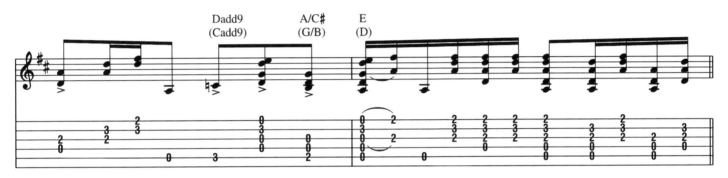

**Artist:** The Beatles

**Album:** *Rubber Soul*

**Year:** 1965

**Guitarists:** John Lennon, George Harrison

**Trivia:** "Norwegian Wood" features a sitar part played by George Harrison, which was the first time the instrument was used on a rock recording.

# Pink Houses

**Words and Music by John Mellencamp**

Track 22

Open G tuning:
(low to high) D–G–D–G–B–D

**Intro**
Moderately ♩ = 114

| | |
|---|---|
| **Artist:** John "Cougar" Mellencamp<br>**Album:** *Uh-Huh*<br>**Year:** 1983<br>**Guitarist:** Mike Wanchic, Larry Crane | **Trivia:** Mellencamp's success with *American Fool* allowed him to add his true last name to his stage moniker for the release of the *Uh-Huh* album. The name "Cougar" was given to him against his will by his first manager Tony DeFries. |

# Wake Up Little Susie

**Words and Music by Boudleaux Bryant and Felice Bryant**

Track 26

**Intro**
Moderate Country ♩ = 96

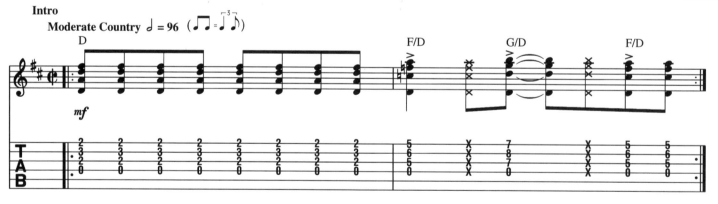

| | |
|---|---|
| **Artist:** The Everly Brothers<br>**Album:** *The Everly Brothers*<br>**Year:** 1958<br>**Guitarists:** Don Everly, Phil Everly | **Trivia:** This song, which achieved the unbelievable feat of topping the Pop, Country, and R&B charts, is George W. Bush's favorite song. |

# Silent Lucidity

**Words and Music by Chris DeGarmo**

**Track 23**

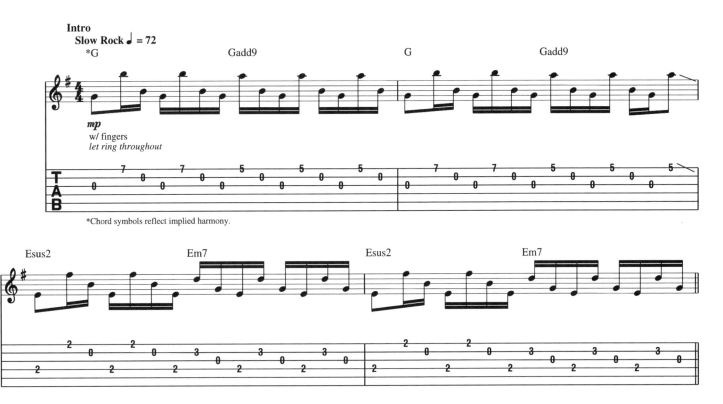

*Chord symbols reflect implied harmony.

**Artist:** Queensryche

**Album:** *Empire*

**Year:** 1990

**Guitarists:** Chris DeGarmo, Michael Wilton

**Trivia:** Though *Empire* was the band's highest-selling album, the follow up, *Promised Land*, peaked on the album charts at #3 (*Empire* peaked at #7.)

# Tears in Heaven

**Words and Music by Eric Clapton and Will Jennings**

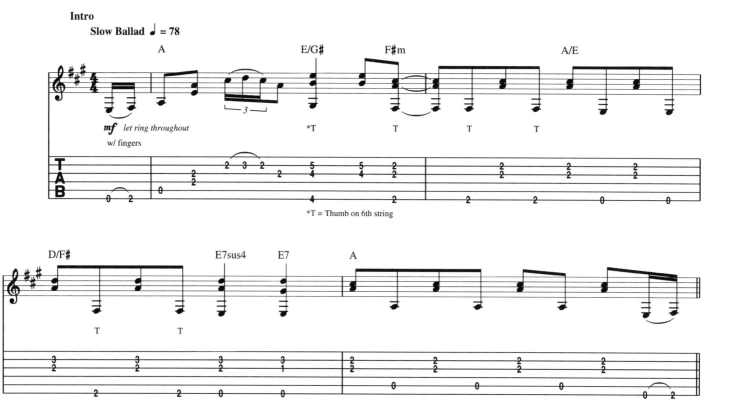

| | |
|---|---|
| **Artist:** Eric Clapton<br>**Album:** *Rush* (motion picture soundtrack), *Unplugged*<br>**Year:** 1992<br>**Guitarist:** Eric Clapton | **Trivia:** It is well-known that this song was written about the death of Clapton's son, Conor. However, Clapton also wrote other songs about his loss, including "Circus" and "Lonely Stranger." |

# Time in a Bottle

**Words and Music by Jim Croce**

**Track 25**

**Artist:** Jim Croce
**Album:** *You Don't Mess Around with Jim*
**Year:** 1972
**Guitarists:** Jim Croce, Maury Muehleisen

**Trivia:** This #1 song wasn't released as a single until after Croce's death. Both Croce and his guitarist, Maury Muehleisen, died in the same tragic plane crash in 1973.

# Wanted Dead or Alive

**Words and Music by Jon Bon Jovi and Richie Sambora**

| | |
|---|---|
| **Artist:** Bon Jovi<br>**Album:** *Slippery When Wet*<br>**Year:** 1986<br>**Guitarist:** Richie Sambora | **Trivia:** This song is the theme song to the television shows *Wanted* and *Dog the Bounty Hunter*, as well as the 1989 film *Young Guns*. |

# When the Children Cry

### Words and Music by Mike Tramp and Vito Bratta

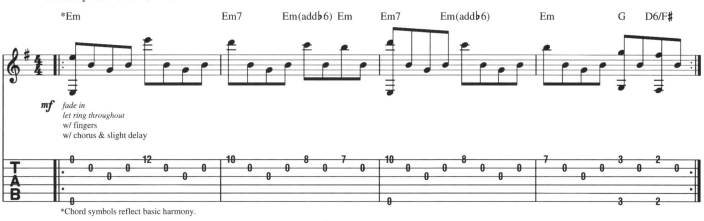

*Chord symbols reflect basic harmony.

**Artist:** White Lion
**Album:** *Pride*
**Year:** 1987
**Guitarist:** Vito Bratta

**Trivia:** In 1986, White Lion had a small role in the Tom Hanks film *The Money Pit*, where the band had a fictitious female member.

---

# You Were Meant for Me

### Lyrics by Jewel Kilcher
### Music by Jewel Kilcher and Steve Poltz

Tune down 1/2 step:
(low to high) Eb–Ab–Db–Gb–Bb–Eb

* slight vibrato

**Artist:** Jewel
**Album:** *Pieces of You*
**Year:** 1995
**Guitarist:** Jewel Kilcher

**Trivia:** *Pieces of You* was mostly recorded live in the studio, so this song and the other singles from the album were re-recorded for the single versions. It is, however, one of the most successful debuts ever, selling 12 million in the U.S. alone.

# The World I Know

**Words and Music by Ed Roland and Ross Brian Childress**

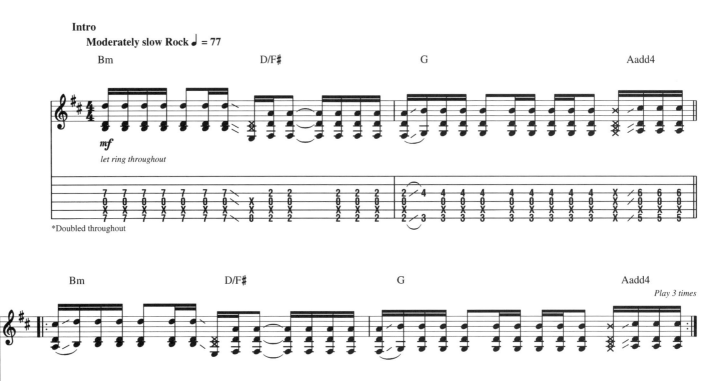

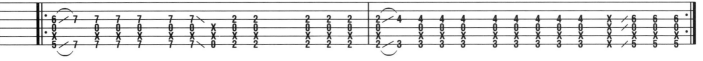

**Artist:** Collective Soul

**Album:** *Collective Soul*

**Year:** 1995

**Guitarists:** Ross Childress, Dean Roland, Ed Roland

**Trivia:** Due to their lyrics, which can be spiritual in nature, this band has been called a Christian rock band (which they deny). Their name, however, comes from a line in Objectivist Ayn Rand's novel *The Fountainhead*.

# Guitar Notation Legend

Guitar Music can be notated three different ways: on a *musical staff*, in *tablature*, and in *rhythm slashes*.

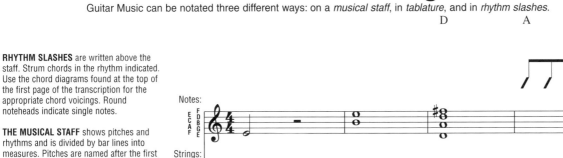

**RHYTHM SLASHES** are written above the staff. Strum chords in the rhythm indicated. Use the chord diagrams found at the top of the first page of the transcription for the appropriate chord voicings. Round noteheads indicate single notes.

**THE MUSICAL STAFF** shows pitches and rhythms and is divided by bar lines into measures. Pitches are named after the first seven letters of the alphabet.

**TABLATURE** graphically represents the guitar fingerboard. Each horizontal line represents a string, and each number represents a fret.

4th string, 2nd fret / 1st & 2nd strings open, played together / open D chord

---

**HALF-STEP BEND:** Strike the note and bend up 1/2 step.

**WHOLE-STEP BEND:** Strike the note and bend up one step.

**GRACE NOTE BEND:** Strike the note and immediately bend up as indicated.

**SLIGHT (MICROTONE) BEND:** Strike the note and bend up 1/4 step.

---

**BEND AND RELEASE:** Strike the note and bend up as indicated, then release back to the original note. Only the first note is struck.

**PRE-BEND:** Bend the note as indicated, then strike it.

**VIBRATO:** The string is vibrated by rapidly bending and releasing the note with the fretting hand.

**WIDE VIBRATO:** The pitch is varied to a greater degree by vibrating with the fretting hand.

---

**HAMMER-ON:** Strike the first (lower) note with one finger, then sound the higher note (on the same string) with another finger by fretting it without picking.

**PULL-OFF:** Place both fingers on the notes to be sounded. Strike the first note and without picking, pull the finger off to sound the second (lower) note.

**LEGATO SLIDE:** Strike the first note and then slide the same fret-hand finger up or down to the second note. The second note is not struck.

**SHIFT SLIDE:** Same as legato slide, except the second note is struck.

---

**TRILL:** Very rapidly alternate between the notes indicated by continuously hammering on and pulling off.

**TAPPING:** Hammer ("tap") the fret indicated with the pick-hand index or middle finger and pull off to the note fretted by the fret hand.

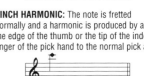

**NATURAL HARMONIC:** Strike the note while the fret-hand lightly touches the string directly over the fret indicated.

Harm.

**PINCH HARMONIC:** The note is fretted normally and a harmonic is produced by adding the edge of the thumb or the tip of the index finger of the pick hand to the normal pick attack.

P.H.

---

**PICK SCRAPE:** The edge of the pick is rubbed down (or up) the string, producing a scratchy sound.

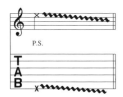

P.S.

**MUFFLED STRINGS:** A percussive sound is produced by laying the fret hand across the string(s) without depressing, and striking them with the pick hand.

**PALM MUTING:** The note is partially muted by the pick hand lightly touching the string(s) just before the bridge.

P.M.

**RAKE:** Drag the pick across the strings indicated with a single motion.

rake

---

**TREMOLO PICKING:** The note is picked as rapidly and continuously as possible.

**VIBRATO BAR DIVE AND RETURN:** The pitch of the note or chord is dropped a specified number of steps (in rhythm) then returned to the original pitch.

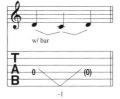

w/ bar

**VIBRATO BAR SCOOP:** Depress the bar just before striking the note, then quickly release the bar.

w/ bar

**VIBRATO BAR DIP:** Strike the note and then immediately drop a specified number of steps, then release back to the original pitch.

w/ bar

# GUITAR RECORDED VERSIONS®

*Guitar Recorded Versions® are note-for-note transcriptions of guitar music taken directly off recordings. This series, one of the most popular in print today, features some of the greatest guitar players and groups from blues and rock to country and jazz.*

*Guitar Recorded Versions are transcribed by the best transcribers in the business. Every book contains notes and tablature.*

AUTHENTIC TRANSCRIPTIONS WITH NOTES AND TABLATURE

| | | |
|---|---|---|
| 00690016 | Will Ackerman Collection | $19.95 |
| 00690501 | Bryan Adams – Greatest Hits | $19.95 |
| 00690002 | Aerosmith – Big Ones | $24.95 |
| 00692015 | Aerosmith – Greatest Hits | $22.95 |
| 00690603 | Aerosmith – O Yeah! (Ultimate Hits) | $24.95 |
| 00690147 | Aerosmith – Rocks | $19.95 |
| 00690146 | Aerosmith – Toys in the Attic | $19.95 |
| 00690139 | Alice in Chains | $19.95 |
| 00690178 | Alice in Chains – Acoustic | $19.95 |
| 00694865 | Alice in Chains – Dirt | $19.95 |
| 00660225 | Alice in Chains – Facelift | $19.95 |
| 00694925 | Alice in Chains – Jar of Flies/Sap | $19.95 |
| 00690387 | Alice in Chains – Nothing Safe: Best of the Box | $19.95 |
| 00690812 | All American Rejects – Move Along | $19.95 |
| 00694932 | Allman Brothers Band – Definitive Collection for Guitar Volume 1 | $24.95 |
| 00694933 | Allman Brothers Band – Definitive Collection for Guitar Volume 2 | $24.95 |
| 00694934 | Allman Brothers Band – Definitive Collection for Guitar Volume 3 | $24.95 |
| 00690755 | Alter Bridge – One Day Remains | $19.95 |
| 00690571 | Trey Anastasio | $19.95 |
| 00690158 | Chet Atkins – Almost Alone | $19.95 |
| 00694876 | Chet Atkins – Contemporary Styles | $19.95 |
| 00694878 | Chet Atkins – Vintage Fingerstyle | $19.95 |
| 00690418 | Best of Audio Adrenaline | $17.95 |
| 00690609 | Audioslave | $19.95 |
| 00690804 | Audioslave – Out of Exile | $19.95 |
| 00694918 | Randy Bachman Collection | $22.95 |
| 00690366 | Bad Company – Original Anthology – Book 1 | $19.95 |
| 00690367 | Bad Company – Original Anthology – Book 2 | $19.95 |
| 00690503 | Beach Boys – Very Best of | $19.95 |
| 00694929 | Beatles: 1962-1966 | $24.95 |
| 00694930 | Beatles: 1967-1970 | $24.95 |
| 00690489 | Beatles – 1 | $24.95 |
| 00694880 | Beatles – Abbey Road | $19.95 |
| 00690110 | Beatles – Book 1 (White Album) | $19.95 |
| 00690111 | Beatles – Book 2 (White Album) | $19.95 |
| 00694832 | Beatles – For Acoustic Guitar | $22.95 |
| 00690137 | Beatles – A Hard Day's Night | $16.95 |
| 00690482 | Beatles – Let It Be | $16.95 |
| 00694891 | Beatles – Revolver | $19.95 |
| 00694914 | Beatles – Rubber Soul | $19.95 |
| 00694863 | Beatles – Sgt. Pepper's Lonely Hearts Club Band | $19.95 |
| 00690383 | Beatles – Yellow Submarine | $19.95 |
| 00690792 | Beck – Guero | $19.95 |
| 00690175 | Beck – Odelay | $17.95 |
| 00690346 | Beck – Mutations | $19.95 |
| 00690632 | Beck – Sea Change | $19.95 |
| 00694884 | Best of George Benson | $19.95 |
| 00692385 | Chuck Berry | $19.95 |
| 00690149 | Black Sabbath | $14.95 |
| 00690148 | Black Sabbath – Master of Reality | $14.95 |
| 00690142 | Black Sabbath – Paranoid | $14.95 |
| 00692200 | Black Sabbath – We Sold Our Soul for Rock 'N' Roll | $19.95 |
| 00690115 | Blind Melon – Soup | $19.95 |
| 00690674 | Blink-182 | $19.95 |
| 00690305 | Blink-182 – Dude Ranch | $19.95 |
| 00690389 | Blink-182 – Enema of the State | $19.95 |
| 00690523 | Blink-182 – Take Off Your Pants and Jacket | $19.95 |
| 00690028 | Blue Oyster Cult – Cult Classics | $19.95 |
| 00690008 | Bon Jovi – Cross Road | $19.95 |
| 00690491 | Best of David Bowie | $19.95 |
| 00690583 | Box Car Racer | $19.95 |
| 00690764 | Breaking Benjamin – We Are Not Alone | $19.95 |
| 00690451 | Jeff Buckley Collection | $24.95 |
| 00690364 | Cake – Songbook | $19.95 |
| 00690564 | The Calling – Camino Palmero | $19.95 |
| 00690261 | Carter Family Collection | $19.95 |
| 00690293 | Best of Steven Curtis Chapman | $19.95 |
| 00690043 | Best of Cheap Trick | $19.95 |
| 00690171 | Chicago – The Definitive Guitar Collection | $22.95 |
| 00690567 | Charlie Christian – The Definitive Collection | $19.95 |
| 00690590 | Eric Clapton – Anthology | $29.95 |
| 00692391 | Best of Eric Clapton – 2nd Edition | $22.95 |
| 00690393 | Eric Clapton – Selections from Blues | $19.95 |
| 00690074 | Eric Clapton – Cream of Clapton | $24.95 |
| 00690265 | Eric Clapton – E.C. Was Here | $19.95 |
| 00690010 | Eric Clapton – From the Cradle | $19.95 |
| 00690716 | Eric Clapton – Me and Mr. Johnson | $19.95 |
| 00690263 | Eric Clapton – Slowhand | $19.95 |
| 00694873 | Eric Clapton – Timepieces | $19.95 |
| 00694869 | Eric Clapton – Unplugged | $22.95 |
| 00690415 | Clapton Chronicles – Best of Eric Clapton | $18.95 |
| 00694896 | John Mayall/Eric Clapton – Bluesbreakers | $19.95 |
| 00690162 | Best of The Clash | $19.95 |
| 00690682 | Coldplay – Live in 2003 | $19.95 |
| 00690494 | Coldplay – Parachutes | $19.95 |
| 00690593 | Coldplay – A Rush of Blood to the Head | $19.95 |
| 00690806 | Coldplay – X & Y | $19.95 |
| 00694940 | Counting Crows – August & Everything After | $19.95 |
| 00690197 | Counting Crows – Recovering the Satellites | $19.95 |
| 00690405 | Counting Crows – This Desert Life | $19.95 |
| 00694840 | Cream – Disraeli Gears | $19.95 |
| 00690285 | Cream – Those Were the Days | $17.95 |
| 00690401 | Creed – Human Clay | $19.95 |
| 00690352 | Creed – My Own Prison | $19.95 |
| 00690551 | Creed – Weathered | $19.95 |
| 00690648 | Very Best of Jim Croce | $19.95 |
| 00690572 | Steve Cropper – Soul Man | $19.95 |
| 00690613 | Best of Crosby, Stills & Nash | $19.95 |
| 00690777 | Crossfade | $19.95 |
| 00699521 | The Cure – Greatest Hits | $24.95 |
| 00690637 | Best of Dick Dale | $19.95 |
| 00690184 | dc Talk – Jesus Freak | $19.95 |
| 00690289 | Best of Deep Purple | $17.95 |
| 00694831 | Derek and The Dominos – Layla & Other Assorted Love Songs | $19.95 |
| 00690384 | Best of Ani DiFranco | $19.95 |
| 00690322 | Ani DiFranco – Little Plastic Castle | $19.95 |
| 00690380 | Ani DiFranco – Up Up Up Up Up Up | $19.95 |
| 00690191 | Dire Straits – Money for Nothing | $24.95 |
| 00695382 | Very Best of Dire Straits – Sultans of Swing | $19.95 |
| 00660178 | Willie Dixon – Master Blues Composer | $24.95 |
| 00690347 | The Doors – Anthology | $22.95 |
| 00690348 | The Doors – Essential Guitar Collection | $16.95 |
| 00690250 | Best of Duane Eddy | $16.95 |
| 00690533 | Electric Light Orchestra Guitar Collection | $19.95 |
| 00690555 | Best of Melissa Etheridge | $19.95 |
| 00690524 | Melissa Etheridge – Skin | $19.95 |
| 00690496 | Best of Everclear | $19.95 |
| 00690515 | Extreme II – Pornograffitti | $19.95 |
| 00690810 | Fall Out Boy – From Under the Cork Tree | $19.95 |
| 00690664 | Best of Fleetwood Mac | $19.95 |
| 00690734 | Franz Ferdinand | $19.95 |
| 00694920 | Best of Free | $19.95 |
| 00690257 | John Fogerty – Blue Moon Swamp | $19.95 |
| 00690089 | Foo Fighters | $19.95 |
| 00690235 | Foo Fighters – The Colour and the Shape | $19.95 |
| 00690808 | Foo Fighters – In Your Honor | $19.95 |
| 00690595 | Foo Fighters – One by One | $19.95 |
| 00690394 | Foo Fighters – There Is Nothing Left to Lose | $19.95 |
| 00690222 | G3 Live – Joe Satriani, Steve Vai, and Eric Johnson | $22.95 |
| 00694807 | Danny Gatton – 88 Elmira St | $19.95 |
| 00690438 | Genesis Guitar Anthology | $19.95 |
| 00120167 | Godsmack | $19.95 |
| 00690753 | Best of Godsmack | $19.95 |
| 00690127 | Goo Goo Dolls – A Boy Named Goo | $19.95 |
| 00690338 | Goo Goo Dolls – Dizzy Up the Girl | $19.95 |
| 00690576 | Goo Goo Dolls – Gutterflower | $19.95 |
| 00690773 | Good Charlotte – Chronicles of Life and Death | $19.95 |
| 00690601 | Good Charlotte – The Young and the Hopeless | $19.95 |
| 00690117 | John Gorka Collection | $19.95 |
| 00690591 | Patty Griffin – Guitar Collection | $19.95 |
| 00690114 | Buddy Guy Collection Vol. A-J | $22.95 |
| 00690193 | Buddy Guy Collection Vol. L-Y | $22.95 |
| 00690697 | Best of Jim Hall | $19.95 |
| 00694798 | George Harrison Anthology | $19.95 |
| 00690778 | Hawk Nelson – Letters to the President | $19.95 |
| 00690068 | Return of the Hellecasters | $19.95 |
| 00692930 | Jimi Hendrix – Are You Experienced? | $24.95 |
| 00692931 | Jimi Hendrix – Axis: Bold As Love | $22.95 |
| 00690304 | Jimi Hendrix – Band of Gypsys | $19.95 |
| 00690321 | Jimi Hendrix – BBC Sessions | $22.95 |
| 00690608 | Jimi Hendrix – Blue Wild Angel | $24.95 |
| 00694944 | Jimi Hendrix – Blues | $24.95 |
| 00692932 | Jimi Hendrix – Electric Ladyland | $24.95 |
| 00690218 | Jimi Hendrix – First Rays of the Rising Sun | $27.95 |
| 00660099 | Jimi Hendrix – Radio One | $24.95 |
| 00690280 | Jimi Hendrix – South Saturn Delta | $24.95 |
| 00690602 | Jimi Hendrix – Smash Hits | $19.95 |
| 00690017 | Jimi Hendrix – Woodstock | $24.95 |
| 00660029 | Buddy Holly | $19.95 |
| 00660169 | John Lee Hooker – A Blues Legend | $19.95 |
| 00694905 | Howlin' Wolf | $19.95 |
| 00690692 | Very Best of Billy Idol | $19.95 |
| 00690688 | Incubus – A Crow Left of the Murder | $19.95 |
| 00690457 | Incubus – Make Yourself | $19.95 |
| 00690544 | Incubus – Morningview | $19.95 |
| 00690136 | Indigo Girls – 1200 Curfews | $22.95 |
| 00690730 | Alan Jackson – Guitar Collection | $19.95 |
| 00694938 | Elmore James – Master Electric Slide Guitar | $19.95 |
| 00690652 | Best of Jane's Addiction | $19.95 |
| 00690721 | Jet – Get Born | $19.95 |
| 00690684 | Jethro Tull – Aqualung | $19.95 |
| 00690647 | Best of Jewel | $19.95 |
| 00694833 | Billy Joel for Guitar | $19.95 |
| 00690751 | John5 – Vertigo | $19.95 |
| 00660147 | Eric Johnson | $19.95 |
| 00694912 | Eric Johnson – Ah Via Musicom | $19.95 |
| 00690660 | Best of Eric Johnson | $19.95 |
| 00690169 | Eric Johnson – Venus Isle | $22.95 |
| 00690271 | Robert Johnson – The New Transcriptions | $24.95 |
| 00699131 | Best of Janis Joplin | $19.95 |
| 00690427 | Best of Judas Priest | $19.95 |
| 00690651 | Juanes – Exitos de Juanes | $19.95 |
| 00690277 | Best of Kansas | $19.95 |
| 00690742 | The Killers – Hot Fuss | $19.95 |
| 00690504 | Very Best of Albert King | $19.95 |
| 00690073 | B. B. King – 1950-1957 | $24.95 |
| 00690444 | B.B. King & Eric Clapton – Riding with the King | $19.95 |
| 00690134 | Freddie King Collection | $19.95 |
| 00690339 | Best of the Kinks | $19.95 |
| 00690156 | Kiss | $17.95 |
| 00690157 | Kiss – Alive! | $19.95 |
| 00694903 | Best of Kiss for Guitar | $24.95 |
| 00690188 | Mark Knopfler – Golden Heart | $19.95 |
| 00690164 | Mark Knopfler Guitar – Vol. 1 | $19.95 |
| 00690165 | Mark Knopfler Guitar – Vol. 2 | $19.95 |
| 00690163 | Mark Knopfler/Chet Atkins – Neck and Neck | $19.95 |
| 00690780 | Korn – Greatest Hits, Volume 1 | $22.95 |
| 00690377 | Kris Kristofferson Collection | $17.95 |
| 00690658 | Johnny Lang – Long Time Coming | $19.95 |
| 00690614 | Avril Lavigne – Let Go | $19.95 |
| 00690726 | Avril Lavigne – Under My Skin | $19.95 |
| 00690679 | John Lennon – Guitar Collection | $19.95 |
| 00690279 | Ottmar Liebert + Luna Negra – Opium Highlights | $19.95 |
| 00690785 | Best of Limp Bizkit | $19.95 |
| 00690781 | Linkin Park – Hybrid Theory | $22.95 |
| 00690782 | Linkin Park – Meteora | $22.95 |
| 00690783 | Best of Live | $19.95 |
| 00699623 | Best of Chuck Loeb | $19.95 |
| 00690743 | Los Lonely Boys | $19.95 |
| 00690720 | Lostprophets – Start Something | $19.95 |
| 00690525 | Best of George Lynch | $19.95 |
| 00694954 | New Best of Lynyrd Skynyrd | $19.95 |
| 00690577 | Yngwie Malmsteen – Anthology | $24.95 |
| 00694845 | Yngwie Malmsteen – Fire and Ice | $19.95 |
| 00694755 | Yngwie Malmsteen's Rising Force | $19.95 |

| | | |
|---|---|---|
| 00694757 Yngwie Malmsteen – Trilogy | $19.95 | |
| 00690754 Marilyn Manson – Lest We Forget | $19.95 | |
| 00694956 Bob Marley – Legend | $19.95 | |
| 00690075 Bob Marley – Natural Mystic | $19.95 | |
| 00690548 Very Best of Bob Marley & The Wailers – One Love | $19.95 | |
| 00694945 Bob Marley – Songs of Freedom | $24.95 | |
| 00690748 Maroon5 – 1.22.03 Acoustic | $19.95 | |
| 00690657 Maroon5 – Songs About Jane | $19.95 | |
| 00690442 Matchbox 20 – Mad Season | $19.95 | |
| 00690616 Matchbox 20 – More Than You Think You Are | $19.95 | |
| 00690239 Matchbox 20 – Yourself or Someone Like You | $19.95 | |
| 00690283 Best of Sarah McLachlan | $19.95 | |
| 00690382 Sarah McLachlan – Mirrorball | $19.95 | |
| 00690354 Sarah McLachlan – Surfacing | $19.95 | |
| 00120080 Don McLean Songbook | $19.95 | |
| 00694952 Megadeth – Countdown to Extinction | $19.95 | |
| 00690244 Megadeth – Cryptic Writings | $19.95 | |
| 00694951 Megadeth – Rust in Peace | $22.95 | |
| 00694953 Megadeth – Selections from Peace Sells...But Who's Buying? & So Far, So Good...So What! | $22.95 | |
| 00690768 Megadeth – The System Has Failed | $19.95 | |
| 00690495 Megadeth – The World Needs a Hero | $19.95 | |
| 00690011 Megadeth – Youthanasia | $19.95 | |
| 00690505 John Mellencamp Guitar Collection | $19.95 | |
| 00690562 Pat Metheny – Bright Size Life | $19.95 | |
| 00690646 Pat Metheny – One Quiet Night | $19.95 | |
| 00690559 Pat Metheny – Question & Answer | $19.95 | |
| 00690565 Pat Metheny – Rejoicing | $19.95 | |
| 00690558 Pat Metheny Trio – 99>00 | $19.95 | |
| 00690561 Pat Metheny Trio – Live | $22.95 | |
| 00690040 Steve Miller Band Greatest Hits | $19.95 | |
| 00690769 Modest Mouse – Good News for People Who Love Bad News | $19.95 | |
| 00694802 Gary Moore – Still Got the Blues | $19.95 | |
| 00690103 Alanis Morissette – Jagged Little Pill | $19.95 | |
| 00690786 Mudvayne – The End of All Things to Come | $22.95 | |
| 00690787 Mudvayne – L.D. 50 | $22.95 | |
| 00690794 Mudvayne – Lost and Found | $19.95 | |
| 00690448 MxPx – The Ever Passing Moment | $19.95 | |
| 00690500 Ricky Nelson Guitar Collection | $17.95 | |
| 00690722 New Found Glory – Catalyst | $19.95 | |
| 00690345 Best of Newsboys | $17.95 | |
| 00690611 Nirvana | $22.95 | |
| 00694895 Nirvana – Bleach | $19.95 | |
| 00690189 Nirvana – From the Muddy Banks of the Wishkah | $19.95 | |
| 00694913 Nirvana – In Utero | $19.95 | |
| 00694901 Nirvana – Incesticide | $19.95 | |
| 00694883 Nirvana – Nevermind | $19.95 | |
| 00690026 Nirvana – Unplugged in York | $19.95 | |
| 00690739 No Doubt – Rock Steady | $22.95 | |
| 00120112 No Doubt – Tragic Kingdom | $22.95 | |
| 00690273 Oasis – Be Here Now | $19.95 | |
| 00690159 Oasis – Definitely Maybe | $19.95 | |
| 00690121 Oasis – (What's the Story) Morning Glory | $19.95 | |
| 00690226 Oasis – The Other Side of Oasis | $19.95 | |
| 00690358 The Offspring – Americana | $19.95 | |
| 00690485 The Offspring – Conspiracy of One | $19.95 | |
| 00690807 The Offspring – Greatest Hits | $19.95 | |
| 00690204 The Offspring – Ixnay on the Hombre | $17.95 | |
| 00690203 The Offspring – Smash | $18.95 | |
| 00690663 The Offspring – Splinter | $19.95 | |
| 00694847 Best of Ozzy Osbourne | $22.95 | |
| 00694830 Ozzy Osbourne – No More Tears | $19.95 | |
| 00690399 Ozzy Osbourne – The Ozzman Cometh | $19.95 | |
| 00690129 Ozzy Osbourne – Ozzmosis | $22.95 | |
| 00690594 Best of Les Paul | $19.95 | |
| 00690546 P.O.D. – Satellite | $19.95 | |
| 00694855 Pearl Jam – Ten | $19.95 | |
| 00690439 A Perfect Circle – Mer De Noms | $19.95 | |
| 00690661 A Perfect Circle – Thirteenth Step | $19.95 | |
| 00690499 Tom Petty – Definitive Guitar Collection | $19.95 | |
| 00690176 Phish – Billy Breathes | $22.95 | |

| | |
|---|---|
| 00690424 Phish – Farmhouse | $19.95 |
| 00690240 Phish – Hoist | $19.95 |
| 00690331 Phish – Story of the Ghost | $19.95 |
| 00690642 Pillar – Fireproof | $19.95 |
| 00690731 Pillar – Where Do We Go from Here | $19.95 |
| 00690428 Pink Floyd – Dark Side of the Moon | $19.95 |
| 00690299 Best of Elvis: The King of Rock 'n' Roll | $19.95 |
| 00692535 Elvis Presley | $18.95 |
| 00690003 Classic Queen | $24.95 |
| 00694975 Queen – Greatest Hits | $24.95 |
| 00690670 Very Best of Queensryche | $19.95 |
| 00694910 Rage Against the Machine | $19.95 |
| 00690145 Rage Against the Machine – Evil Empire | $19.95 |
| 00690179 Rancid – And Out Come the Wolves | $22.95 |
| 00690426 Best of Ratt | $19.95 |
| 00690055 Red Hot Chili Peppers – Bloodsugarsexmagik | $19.95 |
| 00690584 Red Hot Chili Peppers – By the Way | $19.95 |
| 00690379 Red Hot Chili Peppers – Californication | $19.95 |
| 00690673 Red Hot Chili Peppers – Greatest Hits | $19.95 |
| 00690255 Red Hot Chili Peppers – Mother's Milk | $19.95 |
| 00690090 Red Hot Chili Peppers – One Hot Minute | $22.95 |
| 00690511 Django Reinhardt – The Definitive Collection | $19.95 |
| 00690779 Relient K – MMHMM | $19.95 |
| 00690643 Relient K – Two Lefts Don't Make a Right ... But Three Do | $19.95 |
| 00694899 R.E.M. – Automatic for the People | $19.95 |
| 00690260 Jimmie Rodgers Guitar Collection | $19.95 |
| 00690014 Rolling Stones – Exile on Main Street | $24.95 |
| 00690631 Rolling Stones – Guitar Anthology | $24.95 |
| 00690186 Rolling Stones – Rock & Roll Circus | $19.95 |
| 00690685 David Lee Roth – Eat 'Em and Smile | $19.95 |
| 00690694 David Lee Roth – Guitar Anthology | $24.95 |
| 00690749 Saliva – Survival of the Sickest | $19.95 |
| 00690031 Santana's Greatest Hits | $19.95 |
| 00690796 Very Best of Michael Schenker | $19.95 |
| 00690566 Best of Scorpions | $19.95 |
| 00690604 Bob Seger – Guitar Anthology | $19.95 |
| 00690659 Bob Seger and the Silver Bullet Band – Greatest Hits, Volume 2 | $17.95 |
| 00120105 Kenny Wayne Shepherd – Ledbetter Heights | $19.95 |
| 00690750 Kenny Wayne Shepherd – The Place You're In | $19.95 |
| 00120123 Kenny Wayne Shepherd – Trouble Is | $19.95 |
| 00690196 Silverchair – Freak Show | $19.95 |
| 00690130 Silverchair – Frogstomp | $19.95 |
| 00690357 Silverchair – Neon Ballroom | $19.95 |
| 00690419 Slipknot | $19.95 |
| 00690530 Slipknot – Iowa | $19.95 |
| 00690733 Slipknot – Volume 3 (The Subliminal Verses) | $19.95 |
| 00690691 Smashing Pumpkins Anthology | $19.95 |
| 00690330 Social Distortion – Live at the Roxy | $19.95 |
| 00120004 Best of Steely Dan | $24.95 |
| 00694921 Best of Steppenwolf | $22.95 |
| 00690655 Best of Mike Stern | $19.95 |
| 00694801 Best of Rod Stewart | $22.95 |
| 00694957 Rod Stewart – Unplugged...And Seated | $22.95 |
| 00690021 Sting – Fields of Gold | $19.95 |
| 00694955 Sting for Guitar Tab | $19.95 |
| 00690597 Stone Sour | $19.95 |
| 00690689 Story of the Year – Page Avenue | $19.95 |
| 00690520 Styx Guitar Collection | $19.95 |
| 00120081 Sublime | $19.95 |
| 00690519 SUM 41 – All Killer No Filler | $19.95 |
| 00690771 SUM 41 – Chuck | $19.95 |
| 00690612 SUM 41 – Does This Look Infected? | $19.95 |
| 00690767 Switchfoot – The Beautiful Letdown | $19.95 |
| 00690815 Switchfoot – Nothing Is Sound | $19.95 |
| 00690425 System of a Down | $19.95 |
| 00690799 System of a Down – Mezmerize | $19.95 |
| 00690606 System of a Down – Steal This Album | $19.95 |
| 00690531 System of a Down – Toxicity | $19.95 |
| 00694824 Best of James Taylor | $16.95 |
| 00694887 Best of Thin Lizzy | $19.95 |
| 00690238 Third Eye Blind | $19.95 |

| | |
|---|---|
| 00690671 Three Days Grace | $19.95 |
| 00690738 3 Doors Down – Away from the Sun | $22.95 |
| 00690737 3 Doors Down – The Better Life | $22.95 |
| 00690776 3 Doors Down – Seventeen Days | $19.95 |
| 00690267 311 | $19.95 |
| 00690580 311 – From Chaos | $19.95 |
| 00690269 311 – Grass Roots | $19.95 |
| 00690268 311 – Music | $19.95 |
| 00690665 Thursday – War All the Time | $19.95 |
| 00690030 Toad the Wet Sprocket | $19.95 |
| 00690654 Best of Train | $19.95 |
| 00690233 Merle Travis Collection | $19.95 |
| 00690683 Robin Trower – Bridge of Sighs | $19.95 |
| 00690740 Shania Twain – Guitar Collection | $19.95 |
| 00699191 U2 – Best of: 1980-1990 | $19.95 |
| 00690732 U2 – Best of: 1990-2000 | $19.95 |
| 00690775 U2 – How to Dismantle an Atomic Bomb | $22.95 |
| 00694411 U2 – The Joshua Tree | $19.95 |
| 00690039 Steve Vai – Alien Love Secrets | $24.95 |
| 00690172 Steve Vai – Fire Garden | $24.95 |
| 00690343 Steve Vai – Flex-able Leftovers | $19.95 |
| 00660137 Steve Vai – Passion & Warfare | $24.95 |
| 00690605 Steve Vai – Selections from the Elusive Light and Sound, Volume 1 | $24.95 |
| 00694904 Steve Vai – Sex and Religion | $24.95 |
| 00690392 Steve Vai – The Ultra Zone | $22.95 |
| 00690023 Jimmie Vaughan – Strange Pleasures | $19.95 |
| 00690455 Stevie Ray Vaughan – Blues at Sunrise | $19.95 |
| 00690024 Stevie Ray Vaughan – Couldn't Stand the Weather | $19.95 |
| 00690370 Stevie Ray Vaughan and Double Trouble – The Real Deal: Greatest Hits Volume 2 | $22.95 |
| 00690116 Stevie Ray Vaughan – Guitar Collection | $24.95 |
| 00660136 Stevie Ray Vaughan – In Step | $19.95 |
| 00694879 Stevie Ray Vaughan – In the Beginning | $19.95 |
| 00660058 Stevie Ray Vaughan – Lightnin' Blues '83-'87 | $24.95 |
| 00690036 Stevie Ray Vaughan – Live Alive | $24.95 |
| 00690417 Stevie Ray Vaughan – Live at Carnegie Hall | $19.95 |
| 00690550 Stevie Ray Vaughan and Double Trouble – Live at Montreux 1982 & 1985 | $24.95 |
| 00694835 Stevie Ray Vaughan – The Sky Is Crying | $22.95 |
| 00690025 Stevie Ray Vaughan – Soul to Soul | $19.95 |
| 00690015 Stevie Ray Vaughan – Texas Flood | $19.95 |
| 00694776 Vaughan Brothers – Family Style | $19.95 |
| 00690772 Velvet Revolver – Contraband | $19.95 |
| 00690132 The T-Bone Walker Collection | $19.95 |
| 00694789 Muddy Waters – Deep Blues | $24.95 |
| 00690071 Weezer (The Blue Album) | $19.95 |
| 00690516 Weezer (The Green Album) | $19.95 |
| 00690800 Weezer – Make Believe | $19.95 |
| 00690286 Weezer – Pinkerton | $19.95 |
| 00690447 Best of The Who | $24.95 |
| 00694970 The Who – Definitive Guitar Collection: A-E | $24.95 |
| 00694971 The Who – Definitive Guitar Collection: F-Li | $24.95 |
| 00694972 The Who – Definitive Guitar Collection: Lo-R | $24.95 |
| 00694973 The Who – Definitive Guitar Collection: S-Y | $24.95 |
| 00690640 David Wilcox – Anthology 2000-2003 | $19.95 |
| 00690325 David Wilcox – Collection | $17.95 |
| 00690672 Best of Dar Williams | $19.95 |
| 00690320 Dar Williams Songbook | $17.95 |
| 00690319 Stevie Wonder – Some of the Best | $17.95 |
| 00690596 Best of the Yardbirds | $19.95 |
| 00690710 Yellowcard – Ocean Avenue | $19.95 |
| 00690507 Frank Zappa – Apostrophe | $19.95 |
| 00690443 Frank Zappa – Hot Rats | $19.95 |
| 00690589 ZZ Top – Guitar Anthology | $22.95 |

# HAL•LEONARD GUITAR PLAY•ALONG

This series will help you play your favorite songs quickly and easily. Just follow the tab and listen to the CD to hear how the guitar should sound, and then play along using the separate backing tracks. Mac or PC users can also slow down the tempo without changing pitch by using the CD in their computer. The melody and lyrics are included in the book so that you can sing or simply follow along.

**VOL. 1 – ROCK GUITAR**          00699570 / $14.95
Day Tripper • Message in a Bottle • Refugee • Shattered • Sunshine of Your Love • Takin' Care of Business • Tush • Walk This Way.

**VOL. 2 – ACOUSTIC**          00699569 / $14.95
Angie • Behind Blue Eyes • Best of My Love • Blackbird • Dust in the Wind • Layla • Night Moves • Yesterday.

**VOL. 3 – HARD ROCK**          00699573 / $14.95
Crazy Train • Iron Man • Living After Midnight • Rock You like a Hurricane • Round and Round • Smoke on the Water • Sweet Child O' Mine • You Really Got Me.

**VOL. 4 – POP/ROCK**          00699571 / $14.95
Breakdown • Crazy Little Thing Called Love • Hit Me with Your Best Shot • I Want You to Want Me • Lights • R.O.C.K. in the U.S.A. • Summer of '69 • What I Like About You.

**VOL. 5 – MODERN ROCK**          00699574 / $14.95
Aerials • Alive • Bother • Chop Suey! • Control • Last Resort • Take a Look Around (Theme from *M:I-2*) • Wish You Were Here.

**VOL. 6 – '90S ROCK**          00699572 / $14.95
Are You Gonna Go My Way • Come Out and Play • I'll Stick Around • Know Your Enemy • Man in the Box • Outshined • Smells Like Teen Spirit • Under the Bridge.

**VOL. 7 – BLUES GUITAR**          00699575 / $14.95
All Your Love (I Miss Loving) • Born Under a Bad Sign • Hide Away • I'm Tore Down • I'm Your Hoochie Coochie Man • Pride and Joy • Sweet Home Chicago • The Thrill Is Gone.

**VOL. 8 – ROCK**          00699585 / $14.95
All Right Now • Black Magic Woman • Get Back • Hey Joe • Layla • Love Me Two Times • Won't Get Fooled Again • You Really Got Me.

**VOL. 9 – PUNK ROCK**          00699576 / $14.95
All the Small Things • Fat Lip • Flavor of the Weak • I Feel So • Lifestyles of the Rich and Famous• Say It Ain't So • Self Esteem • (So) Tired of Waiting for You.

**VOL. 10 – ACOUSTIC**          00699586 / $14.95
Here Comes the Sun • Landslide • The Magic Bus • Norwegian Wood (This Bird Has Flown) • Pink Houses • Space Oddity • Tangled Up in Blue • Tears in Heaven.

**VOL. 11 – EARLY ROCK**          00699579 / $14.95
Fun, Fun, Fun • Hound Dog • Louie, Louie • No Particular Place to Go • Oh, Pretty Woman • Rock Around the Clock • Under the Boardwalk • Wild Thing.

**VOL. 12 – POP/ROCK**          00699587 / $14.95
867-5309/Jenny • Every Breath You Take • Money for Nothing • Rebel, Rebel • Run to You • Ticket to Ride • Wonderful Tonight • You Give Love a Bad Name.

**VOL. 13 – FOLK ROCK**          00699581 / $14.95
Annie's Song • Leaving on a Jet Plane • Suite: Judy Blue Eyes • This Land Is Your Land • Time in a Bottle • Turn! Turn! Turn! • You've Got a Friend • You've Got to Hide Your Love Away.

**VOL. 14 – BLUES ROCK**          00699582 / $14.95
Blue on Black • Crossfire • Cross Road Blues (Crossroads) • The House Is Rockin' • La Grange • Move It on Over • Roadhouse Blues • Statesboro Blues.

**VOL. 15 – R&B**          00699583 / $14.95
Ain't Too Proud to Beg • Brick House • Get Ready • I Can't Help Myself • I Got You (I Feel Good) • I Heard It Through the Grapevine • My Girl • Shining Star.

**VOL. 16 – JAZZ**          00699584 / $14.95
All Blues • Bluesette • Footprints • How Insensitive • Misty • Satin Doll • Stella by Starlight • Tenor Madness.

**VOL. 17 – COUNTRY**          00699588 / $14.95
Amie • Boot Scootin' Boogie • Chattahoochee • Folsom Prison Blues • Friends in Low Places • Forever and Ever, Amen • T-R-O-U-B-L-E • Workin' Man Blues.

**VOL. 18 – ACOUSTIC ROCK**          00699577 / $14.95
About a Girl • Breaking the Girl • Drive • Iris • More Than Words • Patience • Silent Lucidity • 3 AM.

**VOL. 19 – SOUL**          00699578 / $14.95
Get Up (I Feel Like Being) a Sex Machine • Green Onions • In the Midnight Hour • Knock on Wood • Mustang Sally • Respect • (Sittin' On) the Dock of the Bay • Soul Man.

**VOL. 20 – ROCKABILLY**          00699580 / $14.95
Be-Bop-A-Lula • Blue Suede Shoes • Hello Mary Lou • Little Sister • Mystery Train • Rock This Town • Stray Cat Strut • That'll Be the Day.

**VOL. 21 – YULETIDE**          00699602 / $14.95
Angels We Have Heard on High • Away in a Manger • Deck the Hall • The First Noel • Go, Tell It on the Mountain • Jingle Bells • Joy to the World • O Little Town of Bethlehem.

**VOL. 22 – CHRISTMAS**          00699600 / $14.95
The Christmas Song • Frosty the Snow Man • Happy Xmas • Here Comes Santa Claus • Jingle-Bell Rock • Merry Christmas, Darling • Rudolph the Red-Nosed Reindeer • Silver Bells.

**VOL. 23 – SURF**          00699635 / $14.95
Let's Go Trippin' • Out of Limits • Penetration • Pipeline • Surf City • Surfin' U.S.A. • Walk Don't Run • The Wedge.

**VOL. 24 – ERIC CLAPTON**          00699649 / $14.95
Badge • Bell Bottom Blues • Change the World • Cocaine • Key to the Highway • Lay Down Sally • White Room • Wonderful Tonight.

**VOL. 25 – LENNON & McCARTNEY**          00699642 / $14.95
Back in the U.S.S.R. • Drive My Car • Get Back • A Hard Day's Night • I Feel Fine • Paperback Writer • Revolution • Ticket to Ride.

**VOL. 26 – ELVIS PRESLEY**          00699643 / $14.95
All Shook Up • Blue Suede Shoes • Don't Be Cruel • Heartbreak Hotel • Hound Dog • Jailhouse Rock • Little Sister • Mystery Train.

**VOL. 27 – DAVID LEE ROTH**          00699645 / $14.95
Ain't Talkin' 'Bout Love • Dance the Night Away • Hot for Teacher • Just Like Paradise • A Lil' Ain't Enough • Runnin' with the Devil • Unchained • Yankee Rose.

**VOL. 28 – GREG KOCH**          00699646 / $14.95
Chief's Blues • Death of a Bassman • Dylan the Villain • The Grip • Holy Grail • Spank It • Tonus Diabolicus • Zoiks.

**VOL. 29 – BOB SEGER**          00699647 / $14.95
Against the Wind • Betty Lou's Gettin' Out Tonight • Hollywood Nights • Mainstreet • Night Moves • Old Time Rock & Roll • Rock and Roll Never Forgets • Still the Same.

**VOL. 30 – KISS**          00699644 / $14.95
Cold Gin • Detroit Rock City • Deuce • Firehouse • Heaven's on Fire • Love Gun • Rock and Roll All Nite • Shock Me.

**VOL. 31 – CHRISTMAS HITS**          00699652 / $14.95
Blue Christmas • Do You Hear What I Hear • Happy Holiday • I Saw Mommy Kissing Santa Claus • I'll Be Home for Christmas • Let It Snow! Let It Snow! Let It Snow! • Little Saint Nick • Snowfall.

**VOL. 32 – THE OFFSPRING**          00699653 / $14.95
Bad Habit • Come Out and Play • Gone Away • Gotta Get Away • Hit That • The Kids Aren't Alright • Pretty Fly (For a White Guy) • Self Esteem.

**VOL. 33 – ACOUSTIC CLASSICS**          00699656 / $14.95
Across the Universe • Babe, I'm Gonna Leave You • Crazy on You • Heart of Gold • Hotel California • I'd Love to Change the World • Thick As a Brick • Wanted Dead or Alive.

**VOL. 34 – CLASSIC ROCK**          00699658 / $14.95
Aqualung • Born to Be Wild • The Boys Are Back in Town • Brown Eyed Girl • Reeling in the Years • Rock'n Me • Rocky Mountain Way • Sweet Emotion.

**VOL. 35 – HAIR METAL**          00699660 / $14.95
Decadence Dance • Don't Treat Me Bad • Down Boys • Seventeen • Shake Me • Up All Night • Wait • Talk Dirty to Me.

**VOL. 36 – SOUTHERN ROCK**          00699661 / $14.95
Can't You See • Flirtin' with Disaster • Hold on Loosely • Jessica • Mississippi Queen • Ramblin' Man • Sweet Home Alabama • What's Your Name.

**VOL. 37 – ACOUSTIC METAL**          00699662 / $14.95
Every Rose Has Its Thorn • Fly to the Angels • Hole Hearted • Love Is on the Way • Love of a Lifetime • Signs • To Be with You • When the Children Cry.

**VOL. 38 – BLUES**          00699663 / $14.95
Boom Boom • Cold Shot • Crosscut Saw • Everyday I Have the Blues • Frosty • Further On up the Road • Killing Floor • Texas Flood.

**VOL. 39 – '80S METAL**          00699664 / $14.95
Bark at the Moon • Big City Nights • Breaking the Chains • Cult of Personality • Lay It Down • Living on a Prayer • Panama • Smokin' in the Boys Room.

**VOL. 40 – INCUBUS**          00699668 / $14.95
Are You In? • Drive • Megalomaniac • Nice to Know You • Pardon Me • Stellar • Talk Shows on Mute • Wish You Were Here.

**VOL. 41 – ERIC CLAPTON**          00699669 / $14.95
After Midnight • Can't Find My Way Home • Forever Man • I Shot the Sheriff • I'm Tore Down • Pretending • Running on Faith • Tears in Heaven.

**VOL. 42 – CHART HITS**          00699670 / $14.95
Are You Gonna Be My Girl • Heaven • Here Without You • I Believe in a Thing Called Love • Just Like You • Last Train Home • This Love • Until the Day I Die.

**VOL. 43 – LYNYRD SKYNYRD**          00699681 / $14.95
Don't Ask Me No Questions • Free Bird • Gimme Three Steps • I Know a Little • Saturday Night Special • Sweet Home Alabama • That Smell • You Got That Right.

**VOL. 44 – JAZZ**          00699689 / $14.95
I Remember You • I'll Remember April • Impressions • In a Mellow Tone • Moonlight in Vermont • On a Slow Boat to China • Things Ain't What They Used to Be • Yesterdays.

**VOL. 46 – MAINSTREAM ROCK**          00699722 / $14.95
Just a Girl • Keep Away • Kryptonite • Lightning Crashes • 1979 • One Step Closer • Scar Tissue • Torn.

**VOL. 47 – HENDRIX SMASH HITS**          00699723/ $16.95
All Along the Watchtower • Can You See Me? • Crosstown Traffic • Fire • Foxey Lady • Hey Joe • Manic Depression • Purple Haze • Red House • Remember • Stone Free • The Wind Cries Mary.

**VOL. 48 – AEROSMITH CLASSICS**          00699724 / $14.95
Back in the Saddle • Draw the Line • Dream On • Last Child • Mama Kin • Same Old Song & Dance • Sweet Emotion • Walk This Way.

**VOL. 50 – NÜ METAL**          00699726 / $14.95
Duality • Here to Stay • In the End • Judith • Nookie • So Cold • Toxicity • Whatever.

**VOL. 51 – ALTERNATIVE '90S**          00699727 / $14.95
Alive • Cherub Rock • Come As You Are • Give It Away • Jane Says • No Excuses • No Rain • Santeria.

**VOL. 56 – FOO FIGHTERS**          00699749 / $14.95
All My Life • Best of You • DOA • I'll Stick Around • Learn to Fly • Monkey Wrench • My Hero • This Is a Call.

**VOL. 57 – SYSTEM OF A DOWN**          00699751 / $14.95
Aerials • B.Y.O.B. • Chop Suey! • Innervision • Question! • Spiders • Sugar • Toxicity.

*Prices, contents, and availability subject to change without notice.*

FOR MORE INFORMATION, SEE YOUR LOCAL MUSIC DEALER, OR WRITE TO:

**HAL•LEONARD® CORPORATION**
7777 W. BLUEMOUND RD. P.O. BOX 13819 MILWAUKEE, WI 53213

**Visit Hal Leonard online at www.halleonard.com**

0106

# GUITAR BIBLES

*from*  **HAL•LEONARD®**

*Hal Leonard proudly presents the Guitar Bible series. Each volume contains great songs in authentic, note-for-note transcriptions with lyrics and tablature.*

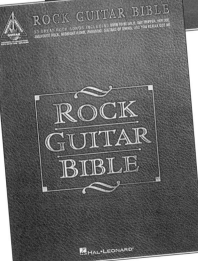

### ACOUSTIC GUITAR BIBLE
35 acoustic classics: Angie • Building a Mystery • Change the World • Dust in the Wind • Hold My Hand • Iris • Maggie May • Southern Cross • Tears in Heaven • Wild World • and more.
00690432.................................................$19.95

### ACOUSTIC ROCK GUITAR BIBLE
35 classics: And I Love Her • Behind Blue Eyes • Come to My Window • Free Fallin' • Give a Little Bit • More Than Words • Night Moves • Pink Houses • Slide • 3 AM • and more.
00690625.................................................$19.95

### BABY BOOMER'S GUITAR BIBLE
35 songs: Angie • Can't Buy Me Love • Happy Together • Hey Jude • Imagine • Laughing • Longer • My Girl • New Kid in Town • Rebel, Rebel • Wild Thing • and more.
00690412.................................................$19.95

### BLUES GUITAR BIBLE
35 blues tunes: Boom Boom • Hide Away • I Can't Quit You Baby • I'm Your Hoochie Coochie Man • Killing Floor • Pride and Joy • Sweet Little Angel • The Thrill Is Gone • and more.
00690437.................................................$19.95

### BLUES-ROCK GUITAR BIBLE
35 songs: Cross Road Blues (Crossroads) • Hide Away • The House Is Rockin' • Love Struck Baby • Move It On Over • Piece of My Heart • Statesboro Blues • You Shook Me • more.
00690450.................................................$19.95

### CLASSIC ROCK GUITAR BIBLE
33 essential rock songs: Beast of Burden • Cat Scratch Fever • Double Vision • Free Ride • Hard to Handle • Life in the Fast Lane • The Stroke • Won't Get Fooled Again • and more.
00690662.................................................$19.95

### COUNTRY GUITAR BIBLE
35 country classics: Ain't Goin' Down • Blue Eyes Crying in the Rain • Boot Scootin' Boogie • Friends in Low Places • I'm So Lonesome I Could Cry • T-R-O-U-B-L-E • and more.
00690465.................................................$19.95

### DISCO GUITAR BIBLE
30 stand-out songs from the disco days: Brick House • Disco Inferno • Funkytown • Get Down Tonight • I Love the Night Life • Le Freak • Stayin' Alive • Y.M.C.A. • and more.
00690627.................................................$17.95

### EARLY ROCK GUITAR BIBLE
35 fantastic classics: Blue Suede Shoes • Do Wah Diddy Diddy • Hang On Sloopy • I'm a Believer • Louie, Louie • Oh, Pretty Woman • Surfin' U.S.A. • Twist and Shout • and more.
00690680.................................................$17.95

### FOLK-ROCK GUITAR BIBLE
35 songs: At Seventeen • Blackbird • Fire and Rain • Happy Together • Leaving on a Jet Plane • Our House • Time in a Bottle • Turn! Turn! Turn! • You've Got a Friend • more.
00690464.................................................$19.95

### GRUNGE GUITAR BIBLE
30 songs: All Apologies • Counting Blue Cars • Glycerine • Jesus Christ Pose • Lithium • Man in the Box • Nearly Lost You • Smells like Teen Spirit • This Is a Call • Violet • and more.
00690649.................................................$17.95

### HARD ROCK GUITAR BIBLE
35 songs: Ballroom Blitz • Bang a Gong • Barracuda • Living After Midnight • Rock You like a Hurricane • School's Out • Welcome to the Jungle • You Give Love a Bad Name • more.
00690453.................................................$19.95

### INSTRUMENTAL GUITAR BIBLE
37 great instrumentals: Always with Me, Always with You • Green Onions • Hide Away • Jessica • Linus and Lucy • Perfidia • Satch Boogie • Tequila • Walk Don't Run • and more.
00690514.................................................$19.95

### JAZZ GUITAR BIBLE
31 songs: Body and Soul • In a Sentimental Mood • My Funny Valentine • Nuages • Satin Doll • So What • Star Dust • Take Five • Tangerine • Yardbird Suite • and more.
00690466.................................................$19.95

### MODERN ROCK GUITAR BIBLE
26 rock favorites: Aerials (System of a Down) • Alive (P.O.D.) • Cold Hard Bitch (Jet) • Kryptonite (3 Doors Down) • Like a Stone (Audioslave) • Whatever (Godsmack) • and more.
00690724.................................................$19.95

### NÜ METAL GUITAR BIBLE
25 edgy metal hits: Aenema • Black • Edgecrusher • Last Resort • People of the Sun • Schism • Southtown • Take a Look Around • Toxicity • Youth of the Nation • and more.
00690569.................................................$19.95

### POP/ROCK GUITAR BIBLE
35 pop hits: Change the World • Heartache Tonight • Money for Nothing • Mony, Mony • Pink Houses • Smooth • Summer of '69 • 3 AM • What I Like About You • and more.
00690517.................................................$19.95

### R&B GUITAR BIBLE
35 R&B classics: Brick House • Fire • I Got You (I Feel Good) • Love Rollercoaster • Shining Star • Sir Duke • Super Freak • and more.
00690452.................................................$19.95

### ROCK GUITAR BIBLE
33 songs: All Day and All of the Night • Born to Be Wild • Day Tripper • Hey Joe • Jailhouse Rock • Money • Paranoid • Sultans of Swing • Walk This Way • You Really Got Me • more!
00690313.................................................$19.95

### ROCKABILLY GUITAR BIBLE
31 songs from artists such as Elvis, Buddy Holly and the Brian Setzer Orchestra: Blue Suede Shoes • Hello Mary Lou • Peggy Sue • Rock This Town • Travelin' Man • and more.
00690570.................................................$19.95

### SOUL GUITAR BIBLE
33 songs: Groovin' • I've Been Loving You Too Long • Let's Get It On • My Girl • Respect • Theme from Shaft • Soul Man • and more.
00690506.................................................$19.95

### SOUTHERN ROCK GUITAR BIBLE
25 southern rock classics: Can't You See • Free Bird • Hold On Loosely • La Grange • Midnight Rider • Sweet Home Alabama • and more.
00690723.................................................$19.95

*Prices, contents, and availability subject to change without notice.*

0606

# GUITAR *signature licks*

Signature Licks book/CD packs provide a step-by-step breakdown of "right from the record" riffs, licks, and solos so you can jam along with your favorite bands. They contain performance notes and an overview of each artist's or group's style, with note-for-note transcriptions in notes and tab. The CDs feature full-band demos at both normal and slow speeds.

**BEST OF ACOUSTIC GUITAR**
00695640 ......................................$19.95

**AEROSMITH 1973-1979**
00695106 ......................................$22.95

**AEROSMITH 1979-1998**
00695219 ......................................$22.95

**BEST OF AGGRO-METAL**
00695592 ......................................$19.95

**BEST OF CHET ATKINS**
00695752 ......................................$22.95

**THE BEACH BOYS DEFINITIVE COLLECTION**
00695683 ......................................$22.95

**BEST OF THE BEATLES FOR ACOUSTIC GUITAR**
00695453 ......................................$22.95

**THE BEATLES BASS**
00695283 ......................................$22.95

**THE BEATLES FAVORITES**
00695096 ......................................$24.95

**THE BEATLES HITS**
00695049 ......................................$24.95

**BEST OF GEORGE BENSON**
00695418 ......................................$22.95

**BEST OF BLACK SABBATH**
00695249 ......................................$22.95

**BEST OF BLINK - 182**
00695704 ......................................$22.95

**BEST OF BLUES GUITAR**
00695846 ......................................$19.95

**BLUES GUITAR CLASSICS**
00695177 ......................................$19.95

**BLUES/ROCK GUITAR MASTERS**
00695348 ......................................$19.95

**BEST OF CHARLIE CHRISTIAN**
00695584 ......................................$22.95

**BEST OF ERIC CLAPTON**
00695038 ......................................$24.95

**ERIC CLAPTON – THE BLUESMAN**
00695040 ......................................$22.95

**ERIC CLAPTON – FROM THE ALBUM UNPLUGGED**
00695250 ......................................$24.95

**BEST OF CREAM**
00695251 ......................................$22.95

**DEEP PURPLE – GREATEST HITS**
00695625 ......................................$22.95

**THE BEST OF DEF LEPPARD**
00696516 ......................................$22.95

**THE DOORS**
00695373 ......................................$22.95

**FAMOUS ROCK GUITAR SOLOS**
00695590 ......................................$19.95

**BEST OF FOO FIGHTERS**
00695481 ......................................$22.95

**GREATEST GUITAR SOLOS OF ALL TIME**
00695301 ......................................$19.95

**BEST OF GRANT GREEN**
00695747 ......................................$22.95

**GUITAR INSTRUMENTAL HITS**
00695309 ......................................$19.95

**GUITAR RIFFS OF THE '60S**
00695218 ......................................$19.95

**BEST OF GUNS N' ROSES**
00695183 ......................................$22.95

**HARD ROCK SOLOS**
00695591 ......................................$19.95

**JIMI HENDRIX**
00696560 ......................................$24.95

**HOT COUNTRY GUITAR**
00695580 ......................................$19.95

**BEST OF JAZZ GUITAR**
00695586 ......................................$24.95

**ERIC JOHNSON**
00699317 ......................................$22.95

**ROBERT JOHNSON**
00695264 ......................................$22.95

**THE ESSENTIAL ALBERT KING**
00695713 ......................................$22.95

**B.B. KING – THE DEFINITIVE COLLECTION**
00695635 ......................................$22.95

**THE KINKS**
00695553 ......................................$22.95

**BEST OF KISS**
00699413 ......................................$22.95

**MARK KNOPFLER**
00695178 ......................................$22.95

**BEST OF YNGWIE MALMSTEEN**
00695669 ......................................$22.95

**BEST OF PAT MARTINO**
00695632 ......................................$22.95

**MEGADETH**
00695041 ......................................$22.95

**WES MONTGOMERY**
00695387 ......................................$22.95

**BEST OF NIRVANA**
00695483 ......................................$24.95

**THE OFFSPRING**
00695852 ......................................$24.95

**VERY BEST OF OZZY OSBOURNE**
00695431 ......................................$22.95

**BEST OF JOE PASS**
00695730 ......................................$22.95

**PINK FLOYD – EARLY CLASSICS**
00695566 ......................................$22.95

**THE POLICE**
00695724 ......................................$22.95

**THE GUITARS OF ELVIS**
00696507 ......................................$22.95

**BEST OF QUEEN**
00695097 ......................................$22.95

**BEST OF RAGE AGAINST THE MACHINE**
00695480 ......................................$22.95

**RED HOT CHILI PEPPERS**
00695173 ......................................$22.95

**RED HOT CHILI PEPPERS – GREATEST HITS**
00695828 ......................................$24.95

**BEST OF DJANGO REINHARDT**
00695660 ......................................$22.95

**BEST OF ROCK**
00695884 ......................................$19.95

**BEST OF ROCK 'N' ROLL GUITAR**
00695559 ......................................$19.95

**BEST OF ROCKABILLY GUITAR**
00695785 ......................................$19.95

**THE ROLLING STONES**
00695079 ......................................$22.95

**BEST OF JOE SATRIANI**
00695216 ......................................$22.95

**BEST OF SILVERCHAIR**
00695488 ......................................$22.95

**THE BEST OF SOUL GUITAR**
00695703 ......................................$19.95

**BEST OF SOUTHERN ROCK**
00695703 ......................................$19.95

**ROD STEWART**
00695663 ......................................$22.95

**BEST OF SYSTEM OF A DOWN**
00695788 ......................................$22.95

**STEVE VAI**
00673247 ......................................$22.95

**STEVE VAI – ALIEN LOVE SECRETS: THE NAKED VAMPS**
00695223 ......................................$22.95

**STEVE VAI – FIRE GARDEN: THE NAKED VAMPS**
00695166 ......................................$22.95

**STEVE VAI – THE ULTRA ZONE: NAKED VAMPS**
00695684 ......................................$22.95

**STEVIE RAY VAUGHAN**
00699316 ......................................$24.95

**THE GUITAR STYLE OF STEVIE RAY VAUGHAN**
00695155 ......................................$24.95

**BEST OF THE VENTURES**
00695772 ......................................$19.95

**THE WHO**
00695561 ......................................$22.95

**BEST OF ZZ TOP**
00695738 ......................................$22.95

Complete descriptions and songlists online!

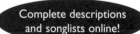

0606